The Geo City Search Guide

By Rich Rano ©
2014

ISBN-13: 978-1502824950

ISBN-10: 1502824957

Preface

The Geo City Search Guide came about when I decided to share what I learned from my own experience.

Having worked in the mortgage industry for several years, and still do to this day, I needed to find a way to get found online.

I was always looking for ways to get my personal website to be found on the first page of major search engines.

After all, finding new clients is not always easy and finding a way to get clients to find me seemed like a great idea.

For several years I struggled to get my website a favorable first page listing on Google.

I discovered that the giant corporations, like Lending Tree, Chase, Wells Fargo, were the people I was in competition with.

Needless to say, their advertising budget and size alone made it difficult for me to compete.

Finally, I discovered the **"secret sauce"** that levels the playing field for us "smaller fish" that want to be found online.

The answer was that by getting found locally, and by adding *"keyword phrases"* like your product or service combined with the cities that you do business in.

Instead of competing for one *"keyword"* "Mortgage" for example, I added "Seattle Mortgage".

This is still a competitive *"keyword phrase"* due to the number of competitors, but I found that by adding more words the competition was lessened. In addition, by adding cities and towns, it lessened the number of competitors.

This strategy gave my website a higher ranking on Google, Yahoo, Bing and other major search engines.

Now, the *"secret sauce"* process is actually a bit more complicated than just adding *"keyword phrases"*, since you also need to add a few more ingredients to make the search engines rank your website higher.

The Geo City Search Guide is designed to guide you through the rest of the necessary steps to help you quickly get high rankings and enjoy the benefits of clients or customers coming to you.

The Geo City Search Guide

Congrats, you have taken the first step to exploding your business.

Here's a fact worth considering: 97 percent of consumers search for local businesses online.

This means that if your business is not listed on the first page of Google, Yahoo or Bing, then you are losing customers.

The Geo City Search Guide is designed to give you step by step instructions on how to get your business listed in the top cities and towns that you want to do business in quickly.

This step by step guide, written for the "do it yourselfer", is designed to help you achieve top search engine rankings in the cities and towns that you offer your products and or services in.

I'm going to show you how to **Geo-Target** your business or service to get more customers.

First, let me start by defining *Geo Targeting:*

Geo targeting or geo marketing also known as **Local SEO** *(search engine optimization)* and internet marketing is the method of determining the geographical location of a website visitor and delivering different content to that visitor based on his or her location, such as country, region, state, city, zip code, etc.

Geo Targeting is a form of **SEO** (search engine optimization) in the sense that you target specific key words to a specific geographic area.

Companies can charge you hundreds even thousands of dollars to do this "*SEO Geo Targeting"* for you, and you will have to pay for these services ongoing.

What my guide does is teach you how to accomplish the same results yourself, for the one time small price you already paid for *The Geo City Search Guide.*

The steps that you will learn will increase your customers/client base by allowing your website or business to be found in the geographic location that they are in.

By you targeting specific cities or geographic areas, your chances of landing on page 1 of **Google** and other search engines greatly increase.

So you win with all that new business you are going to get.

Instead of hunting for customers, they will now find you.

Geo-targeting can be helpful for:

1. Small businesses that want to drive traffic to their physical shops or offices by targeting customers searching online for local providers of goods and services.

2. Service-oriented businesses, such as plumbers or estate agents.

3. Large businesses that want to drive customers to their web sites and/or physical shop locations.

Why is **Geo Targeting** more cost effective and beneficial to your business?

The answer is simple.

When you try to get on the first page of **Google**, etc., with one generic keyword, you are competing with major players and it is very expensive to compete with the major players as a small business owner, real estate agent or insurance agent, etc.

One example of a keyword that I use in my business is the word "Mortgage". If I were to only try to use that one keyword and try to get on page one of **Google**, I would be competing with tens of thousands of other people in my industry. Remember, there are thousands of mortgage companies throughout the United States and the world.

I could use a **"pay per click"** service and pay for the keyword "mortgage".

The last time I checked, every time someone clicks on my paid keyword "mortgage", it would cost me about $50.00 per click.

That is not cost effective and I do not do business in the whole USA.

My chances of getting on the first page of **Google** would be almost impossible.

In addition to that, if I did get customers from far away, I would not even be able to service those customers anyway.

So, by adding to my website content additional "words" or "cities" to that keyword, now making it a "keyword phrase", my chances increase dramatically to land on the first page of Google and other top search engines.

Paid Listings vs. Organic

The "keyword *phrases*" that I refer to are not going to be pay per click. They will be in fact "free" or **"*organic*"** keywords that I will add to my website. More on that subject later.

An example of this type of *"keyword phrase"* would be "Seattle Mortgages" or "Seattle VA Mortgages", which I actually did use and I do get found on page 1 of Google quite frequently.

It really works and it works quickly once you start creating those unique web pages and keyword phrases.

The old advertising methods like newspaper, radio, TV, etc., still work but are not only very expensive but still do not produce the results that being found on page 1 of Google does.

By following the instructions outlined below, you will quickly get new customers that you never thought possible.

The first thing is you will need is a website. If you do not have a website that you are able to create and add web pages then you will need to get one.

If you already have a website that you can add many new pages to, or have a web design service at your disposal, then you can skip to the next page.

Some people already have a website but their webhost or website plan does not allow them to add more pages.

If this is the case, then you will need a webhost that will allow you to have or add several pages.

The number of pages that you want to have depends on how many products and how many cities that you want to target.

If you need a website or web hosting service that you can add several pages to there are several options available to you by doing a search online for Web Hosting companies.

For someone on a limited budget that needs to find a web host service, there are a few affordable ones out there. I use Go Daddy and it allows me hundreds of pages for about $10.00 per month, which is very inexpensive and also very easy to use and get set up quickly.

Go Daddy has a web service called "Web Builder", which means you don't need to know html (that is one of the programming languages that professional web site builders know and use). This means that you don't need to know all of the technical programming language that is normally needed, so most anyone can build a website easily.

It is very user friendly and uses the WSYWIG (what you see is what you get) concept for website design.

There are several templates and color schemes available for you to use.

You will need a Domain name and if you don't have a Domain
Name, you can buy that from Go Daddy as well for a low price.

An example of a Domain Name is a unique web address like yourname.com, or something similar, as long as someone else is not already using the same name.

You can purchase a Domain Name for about $6.00-$12.00 per year. You can purchase that from Go Daddy along with your website, if you

choose.
You can also "Google" web hosting services and domain name services a provider for both.

The Next Step is to start building your website. If you are using Go

Daddy's Web Builder, it won't take long.

You will build your Home Page with content that you want to share. You can add images, and links.

You will then start adding other pages like the "About Us" page, a Contact Page, etc.

There are several samples on their website, along with websites all over the internet you can look at for ideas, pictures, and add links to other websites, etc.

Once you "start" it's not as hard as it may sound, and I have always believed in the old saying that *"starting the job is a job half done"* or something like that.

Now if you already have a website, all the easier.

Assuming you now have a basic "website", then it's time to start adding the pages using the cities, towns and keyword phrases you listed from above.

Once you have built and published your website then you can now work on getting listed in the top cities of your choice for the search terms, or keywords of your choice.

The next step is for you to decide what cities and towns that you want to focus on.

You should make a list of the top 10-12 cities and towns. For example, if your target area is Chicago, you may also want to add many of the surrounding suburbs, Like Des Plaines, etc.

Incorporate Keywords into Your Website Content

The next step is to think of, or you already may know, what

"Search terms" or "keyword phrases", those customers may type in to find the product or services that you offer.

For example let's say you are a realtor who sells homes in
Chicago, a few are examples of some good keyword phrases are:

Homes Chicago, Real Estate Chicago, Home Values Chicago, Real Estate Agents Chicago, Condos Chicago, etc.

We type in keywords when we search for products, services and answers on Google, Yahoo, Bing and other search engines.

You can capture the interest of search engines by assigning keywords to pages of your website.

Doing so is known as "optimizing Your Website". This is where the phrase SEO or Search Engine Optimization comes from.

Chose keywords and Keyword Phrases for your website:

  1. Relevant, which means that the keywords are "what you do or sell" as a business owner.

An example would be that if you are a Realtor in Seattle then you may want to add keyword phrases like houses for sale in Seattle.

2.   **Be Specific,** which means that the more specific your keywords are the less competition and the higher you will rank. Your Keywords should represent what you do, your location your products and services offered, in your specific industry.

3.   **Keep it Natural:** Don't try and overuse your Keywords as search engines read your content like we do. The search engine spiders evaluate context, making sure the content is relevant for the person searching for information.

Then create the same products and services for another city or town nearby. Some examples are:

Homes Palatine, Real Estate Palatine, Home Values Palatine, Real Estate Agents Palatine, Condos Palatine. Etc.

You should try and pick about 10 cities and 10 to 20 services or products. That would give you 200 unique web pages. 10 cities x 20 services= 200 unique pages. In doing so, each time someone types in the *"keyword phrase "*Real Estate Chicago, etc., you will be listed on the search engine they are using.

If you can't come up with that many pages, don't worry, just try to make quite a few combinations and since this is a work in progress you will think of more and more and add the pages as you create them.

This also means that you can always add and improve your website as time goes on.

The more combinations of key word phrases and cities you have, the more business you will get!

Take your time though, so the web pages that you create are somewhat unique from each other and the potential customers get value from your website.

Now if you already have a website, all the easier.

Assuming you now have a basic "website", then it's time to start adding the pages using the cities, towns and keyword phrases you listed from above.

Here are some tips for creating pages for different cities and towns and different "key word search terms"

Creating pages on your site that target specific cities where you want to rank well in the organic search results for local businesses takes a little time and thought, but the rewards are worth it.

Why go after organic rankings when you can get visible in the paid local search results? (AKA Google+Local and Bing Places.) The reason is simple, most people click on the "organic" listings rather than the paid listings.

The ratio is about 75% organic clicks versus 25% paid clicks search listings.

This is also way less expensive for you, as you will not have to fork out hundreds of dollars per month in paid ad's.

Many people will try and simply totally copy the content from one web page and paste on a new web page, simply changing the city name.

Google may catch this and punish you for doing that, therefore making your site very hard to be found.

Differentiating your pages will help you avoid a couple of traps:
(1) Possibly being penalized by Google and (2) annoying and repelling your potential customers.

First start by creating a new page on your website and name it, using the city that you are targeting.

In the same page name add a "keyword phrase".

Create the "Title" of each webpage that you create. An example of a new page title would be: Chicago Wine Tasting

Then, usually on the top of your page you will insert one or two "Headlines" using the same words you used on your page title.

Now you want to use some unique Content in your page.

Content: Some Content examples are:

Write a simple case-study on a job you did in your target city.

Write about what you like about working in your target city, or what you like about its residents.

You could write a blurb or something newsworthy that happened in your target city. Just write something that shows at least a small (but real) connection to that city.

Talk about your "keyword phrases" that you are using and mention the City you are targeting a few times in your paragraph (s).You may want to add links, like click here to see "Wineries in Chicago" for example, or link to "Chicago Tourist Activities" or something of interest to your customers.

Photos; if you don't have pictures of jobs you did in your target city maybe have a picture of a local landmark. Reflect the "local"

Subject matter in the names of the photos, and maybe in the alt tags and title attributes.

Add Videos (more options). Each city page can have a different video. Assuming you're the one who created the videos, you can include in your

YouTube descriptions a link to your city page, and you can geotag the video.

Testimonials; Mention the city of the customers who wrote them. Depending on what your business is and how close you are with your customers, you might also be able to weave in relevant photos.

Add Google Maps; See if you can make a few custom maps that potential customers might find handy.

Once you complete one page with a unique City and Search terms then you can start another.

I would cheat a little by copy and pasting some of the content about the city and add content using the new pages "Keyword Search Terms".

Example, I would take the content from Chicago above, but then add the new Keyword Phrase content, like Chicago Winemaking.

This will help you quickly create several unique pages for each city and Keyword Phrase, and before you know it, you will be ranking high for each of the cities you are targeting.

You can also create pages for the counties and states or regions that you are targeting.

There are other ways that will greatly help you get top listings on major search engines.

One of the best free tools at your disposal is to use Google Places.

Google will allow the business owner or authorized person to add their business on Google Places. Google does not charge for this service and your business gets listed in the city in which you are located.

You can add a picture of your storefront if you are a brick and mortar business and Google also shows where your business is located on a map.

Add your website to Google Places/ Google Maps:

Adding a listing takes just three steps. They are:

1. Submit your information, from basic contact info to photos and video.

2 . Verify your listing by phone or postcard.

3. Wait for your listing to appear on Google.

In Google Maps, you can find a specific business location and add details about that business, such as hours of operation, contact phone number, the website, and more. To add a business "place" to Google Maps, you are required to sign up for Google Places. You will then need to submit information for your "place" and verify your information by telephone or postcard.

Content Marketing

Content marketing is writing copy whose primary purpose attracts and retains customers by consistently creating relevant and valuable content with the intention of helping a consumer make an informed decision based on the facts presented. Basically instead of "pitching" your potential customers, you are educating them by providing them with ongoing valuable information.
This allows you to be the "trusted authority" on the subject of the services or products you are selling.

The strategy is the belief that if we, as businesses, deliver consistent, ongoing valuable information to buyers, they ultimately reward us with their business and loyalty.

The key here is that you are delivering relevant and valuable information rather than flashing banner ads at their face and so the customers will appreciate that.

In addition, since you are using "keywords" and "keyword phrases" in your content marketing, the search engines will pick this up. You will also get more visitors to your website because people will keep coming back for information and may even refer their associates who will also benefit from the information.

Google Hummingbird Algorithm Update:

In 2013, Google made a major change to its algorithm for the first time since 2001. They started using the Hummingbird algorithm. Technically it's accurate to call Google Hummingbird an algorithm update, but it's a major overhaul to the algorithm.

Google Hummingbird and Semantic Search

At the heart of the Hummingbird lies the all-important concept of semantics, or meaning. Even the fanciest computers are still pretty stupid. This is because although it's easy for humans to distinguish between two different yet similar concepts (by virtue of context), computers can't do this unless they're explicitly told.

Selecting Keywords and Keyword Phrases
One very important fact to consider is this: If your keyword or keyword phrase is not being used by other people in your industry, then your chances of coming up on the first page of Google is very high.

The keyword or keyword phrases that you are using are not very competitive, so you have an easy advantage to get your website on the first page of the search engines.

Just put the phrase(s) you want to rank well for in the <title></title> tag and in at least one other area on the page.

An example that I use myself is instead of just putting "home" on my page, I put Seattle Mortgages, or Seattle FHA Mortgages, or Seattle VA Mortgages, depending on the page.

By using these tips, you should get listed within a month on the first page of Google, etc.

If your keyword or keyword phrases are not competitive, then you will have to work harder to compete.

Working harder simply means writing valuable "Quality "content that is useful to your readers.

In that content, you should use your keywords and keyword phrases in a few places on the pages.

Remember, you are not trying to trick the search engines by overloading them with keywords, but by using those keywords in a relevant, meaningful way.

As Google itself says "Focus on the user and all else will follow".

What is considered a "Quality" website page by a search engine?

First, the content on your webpage should be relevant.

The dictionary defines relevant as "having direct bearing on the matter in hand; pertinent.

The page has been around for a while. Obviously, that part will come with time.

Your website in general has a lot of useful information. This comes also with time and the fact that you are building several "quality" pages.

The page is considered an authority on the subject matter.

The links in your webpages are not broken, but actually work and link to other websites.

The page loads quickly. This means that you have "too many" pictures and other aspects that would take it too long to load. Remember, Google wants the user to find their search engine useful, so the user can quickly find the information they are searching.

Backlinks are yet another way to boost your rankings on Google and other search engines.

At its most basic, a link is a connection between any two web pages.

From a search engine optimization perspective, a number of backlinks demonstrate a site's popularity. Essentially, every time a site links to your pages, it's saying that it finds them worthy of sharing with its readers.

There are several ways to create backlinks to your website.

One way is to write valuable content about your products or services and then contact sites linking to similar content and let them know what you've created.

Whether it is your knowledge of your industry, your local area or something else, share it with other people by writing an article for a local periodical or other media. You'll be allowed a byline at the start or end of the article which you can use to link to your site.

To find websites that may be a good source for a backlink, look to your competitor's websites and see what they are linking to.

You can conduct a search for your competitors' URLs at sites such as MajesticSEO or the Open Site Explorer. Once you discover which sites are linking to your competitors, simply visit those sites to find out if your content might be a good fit.

Simply stated, a good backlink is a link that sends traffic to your website.

Building backlinks will take some time to do depending on how creative you are at providing valuable content.

Google Webmaster Tools is another free tool provided to improve and optimize websites by giving a clear picture of exactly what is going on within the site. This free tool is used to drive more traffic and more sales from a website.

Google Analytics

Since Google needs to go into your website (crawl) to get data, it is no surprise that Google will recognize your website on a higher level than if you do not have Google Analytics code embedded.

You will need to paste the Google Analytics code into each page that you want to have it on.

To get the free Google Analytics code you will need to do the following steps:

Sign into your Google account or create a Google account for free.

Google will allow you to get a code that you can copy and paste on to your website, for free.

This code will track your visitors and let you know which keywords they are using to find your website.

Once you have added the code into each of your website pages that you want the code on, you will have many valuable reports at your disposal.

Google Analytics helps you analyze visitor traffic and paint a complete picture of your audience and their needs, wherever they are along the path to purchase.

There is a ton of data available on Google Analytics. You only need to focus on some of the data in order to improve your traffic, or visitors/leads.

Keywords (which keywords and keyword phrases are sending you visitors). When you know which keywords is driving traffic, and then you can optimize your website by using more of these keywords.

Go into your website and infuse more of those keywords that are driving traffic into your content.

Referring Sites (seeing which websites are sending you visitors, like Facebook or Linked In for example).

Knowing this information will allow you to spend more time posting on those websites that are sending you traffic.

There is more information you can track and study from Google Analytics, Some other information available is:

Visitor Overview (new versus returning visitors). This just allows you to track more marketing information that you may find useful.

Content Analysis (tells you what content people are interested in so you can publish more of that valuable information).

So take advantage of Googles Webmaster Tools, as not only it is free to use but they can only help your rankings.

A Word about Metatags

Metadata plays an important role in search engine optimization
(SEO), because it "summarizes" the data for search engines.

Simply stated, it makes finding and linking to website content easier for the search engines.

When you write content for a website, it's important for you to include SEO HTML tags, also called Meta content. . This tells the search engines exactly what your site is about.

Although metadata is not required to have your website listed on search engines, but it also will boost your site's rankings.

Depending on your webhost, these Meta tags can easily be added.

On Go Daddy's Web Builder, it is quite easy to add them with just a few clicks of a mouse.

In ending: there is no end.

I will keep you abreast of updates and will compose more e books, like one for social media marketing.

Search engines are constantly changing their algorithms but if you follow the aforementioned steps your website will surely succeed.

For those of you who prefer that someone else do all the work, or simply do not have the time to create and manage a website and the SEO components, we can do it for you.

It will cost more but the benefits of more customers and more money may outweigh the cost.

Social Media

As you may already know, Social Media is a hot topic and a lot has been written about it on the internet.

I'm not going to talk much about how to use it, as that in itself is another book.

I can tell you that using Facebook, LinkedIn, Twitter and other social media sites will also help you get more exposure and also increase your rankings on the major search engines.

Conversion

Remember that not only it is important to get thousands of unique visitors to your website but also to convert them to prospects or leads or actual sales!

Most marketing experts agree that it takes seven contacts, or "touches", with a prospect in order to convert them into a sale.

So, you will need to "capture" their information, like email or phone number in order to continue to market to them.

There are a few ways to capture their contact information, as you probably have witnessed yourself.

One way is to place a "Join My Mailing List" signup form on your website.

In order for your prospect to be willing to "sign up", you need a direct call to action or a reward for signing up.

A free white paper that gives them tips on challenges pertinent to their specific industry, or a free newsletter is a couple of incentives to build your list of prospects.

Many companies use a service such as "Aweber", which sends out the first email to the prospect, then sends auto responders or follow up emails, automatically after you set it up, so you have a better chance of gaining a new customer.

For more information on their service, visit www.aweber.com.

There are other services like Aweber, but I find them the easiest to use and very affordable.

The first month with AWeber is also free, so you can test and experiment with various auto responder emails.

Automated Service:

There is another option for you to get your website listed on page 1 of Google and other top search engines in the geographical areas that you want to target.

It is an automated service where we will do all the work for you.

We will optimize your web pages and create approximately 200 unique web pages for you in a geographical area that you want to target.

What we do is target app 10 cities and about 20 products or services that you have to offer. You can also use app., 10 products or services in about 10 cities or some similar combination to come up with about 200 pages.

We create these pages on our own server so it does not interfere with your current website and we do all the work.

The service price varies and it is an ongoing fee, so please email me at rcrano.com for more information.

You can also contact me by visiting www.rcrano.com and click on the Contact Us link, or simply email me at rcrano@gmail.com, and I will contact you. Success to you!

www.ingramcontent.com/pod-product-compliance
Lightning Source LLC
Chambersburg PA
CBHW081807170526
45167CB00008B/3367